TIM MILLER

How to Be a Print Broker

(Almost) Everything You Need to Know to Start and Run a Successful Print Broker Business

Copyright © Tim Miller, 2018

All rights reserved. No part of this publication may be reproduced, stored or transmitted in any form or by any means, electronic, mechanical, photocopying, recording, scanning, or otherwise without written permission from the publisher. It is illegal to copy this book, post it to a website, or distribute it by any other means without permission.

Tim Miller has no responsibility for the persistence or accuracy of URLs for external or third-party Internet Websites referred to in this publication and does not guarantee that any content on such Websites is, or will remain, accurate or appropriate.

First edition

*This book was professionally typeset on Reedsy.
Find out more at reedsy.com*

Contents

I   How to Be a Print Broker

Every Print Broker is Different	3
How Print Brokers Make Money	5
Great Expectations ... and Reality	7
What Do Print Brokers Sell?	9
How to Get Paying Clients	11
Finding Your Own Vendors	13
Getting Paid	15
More than Just a Print Broker	17
Quick Start: 10 Steps to Starting Your Print Broker Business	19
Preparing Files for Printing	21

II   Bonus Section: Resources for Print Brokers

Offset Printing	25
Large Format Print Vendors	27
Specialty Printing	29
Software Suggestions	30
Design Resources	31
About the Author	32

I

How to Be a Print Broker

(Almost) Everything You Need to Know to Start and Run a Successful Print Broker Business

1

Every Print Broker is Different

Randy got his start in a print shop — thirty years ago. The technology has changed, the customers have changed, and even the terminology has changed. Although he has a website, he can barely use email, can't design a business card, and makes a good living for his family being the middleman between his clients and the print shop.

Larry is an installer. He doesn't design or print signs, but he sells and installs them. In between his own jobs, he makes money installing for smaller sign shops or independent operators. He has no website, very little overhead, and a great reputation that keeps his clients coming back. His job as a print broker and sign installer provides for his family.

My own story is different as well. I started out as a self-taught graphic designer in 2005, designing business cards and brochures, and ordering my clients' jobs from VistaPrint. Not very long after, I began to discover the wonderful world of wholesale printing. With a business license, I could get 1000 business cards for the same price as 250! I set up a display at a local author's convention for $50, used a science fair tri-fold board and some laminated samples of my work, and gained several clients and jobs. For thirteen years, I have been a print broker.

During that time, I have learned several things I wished I had known in 2005. I made several mistakes I hope you will avoid. And I discovered some "trade secrets" that I think will make your life as a print broker much easier and more rewarding.

This book won't tell you *everything* you need to know about being a print broker, but it will tell you *almost* everything you need to know. And it certainly will tell you most of what I know about being a print broker!

2

How Print Brokers Make Money

Let's cut to the chase. The reason you're considering becoming a print broker is because you want to make money doing it.

A teacher may teach because he loves to teach. An author may write because of passion instead of profit. But nobody becomes a print broker out of a sense of mission. Print brokers are print brokers to make money.

There are three key ways you can make money as a print broker. None of them, by the way, involve actually printing money, which is illegal for nearly everyone reading this book.

A print broker is a middleman between a consumer and a print shop. Another name for a print broker is an independent salesperson who has to pay his own commission.

The first way a print broker can make money is by charging retail markup on wholesale printing prices. You pay the printing company $25 for 500 business cards, but charge the customer $50. You make $25.

Second, a print broker can make money by selling related services as well. Perhaps you can install signs, or design marketing materials. You can make money on both the product and the services. Add a half hour of design time to the $25 business cards, and the $15 profit could turn into $40 profit.

Finally, many print brokers have their clients pay the printing company directly, but receive a commission from their clients for arranging the printing and finding the companies.

In today's economy, where printing is viewed as a commodity, I suggest that you are better off to have set retail fees for the printing (50 to 100% markup) and charge for added services.

3

Great Expectations ... and Reality

If you've come here looking for a get rich quick book, this isn't it. Print brokers work for their living, and although rich, lazy print brokers may exist, I don't know any.

You can make money being a print broker. But to do it, you may initially have to work hard, late, and long to make sales, keep customers, and fulfill needs.

At the same time, print brokers have some scheduling and financial flexibility. They can work from home, or from Panera, or even from a friendly local print shop!

This book will give you the foundation for a successful print broker business, but it is up to you to design and build the structure from the ground up. Just as every broker is different, every business is different.

Here are five things I wished I had known at the beginning of the business:

1. Don't be overly generous. Here's what I would do. I would see a great wholesale price for business cards — "Wow! I can get 1000 business cards for $12?" And then I might offer a customer 1000 business cards for $20 — designed, printed, and shipped. That's a great deal for them, about $30 less than anywhere else, but not a very good deal for me: about $4 per hour of work, when you include marketing, design, and ordering. If there was a mistake and I had to reprint, there was no profit whatsoever.

2. Don't be greedy. Make sure you're providing a good service for your clients and not just taking their money. Some clients are going to be less demanding than others, but give each client your best. Charge what you need to charge, and even enough to make a reasonable profit, but don't overcharge just because you can. "Do unto others as you would have them do unto you."
3. Schedule your time. It's easy to get overwhelmed and not follow up on client requests. Figure out how much time a project should take, and block out the time for it. Flexible scheduling is one thing, but this is not a job you can do in your "spare time" unless you block the time out.
4. Respect your clients. Answer their phone calls and their questions. Tell them when you can't handle a job, and try to refer them to someone when you can. Customer service is key in this business.
5. Double-check every order. If you don't know something for sure, double-check it. Maps, phone numbers, and web addresses must be correct! One of my earliest jobs was a postcard campaign for a private school. I designed a postcard with a roadway and the tagline, "Life is a journey. Get directions." Unfortunately, on the location map, I had the school on the wrong side of the road!

In life, expectations don't always line up with reality. But by taking these simple steps, I hope the reality of your print broker business will exceed your dreams!

4

What Do Print Brokers Sell?

As a print broker, you are selling your knowledge, your experience, and your sources to your customers. If you can't sell something to them, at least direct them to someone who can.

Here are some of the common products print brokers are expected to sell to clients:

- Marketing Materials: brochures, flyers, postcards, business cards, envelopes
- Large Format Printing: signs, banners, vehicle wraps, wall graphics, window graphics
- Promotional Items: custom pens, shirts, kazoos (really?), jump drives
- Specialty Printing: books, newsletters, church bulletins
- Non-printed Marketing Items: websites, digital ad banners, email newsletter templates
- Services: direct mail services, sign installation and fabrication, marketing strategies

Of course, I would recommend offering the simple stuff at first — mostly the first two categories.

But print brokers sell more than individual products and services. Print brokers sell solutions. When you're interacting with clients, ask about their business. Ask about their customers. Ask about their strengths and weaknesses. Find ways to solve their problems, and you will get their business.

5

How to Get Paying Clients

After you change your LinkedIn profile to reflect your new business, you're going to be inundated with clients. Your uncle needs a decal for the back of his pickup truck. Your mom needs a banner for Joey's kindergarten graduation open house. Your next door neighbor needs a yard sign to keep the kids of the grass. And this really great charity is willing to give you a lot of exposure if you'll donate a thousand brochures to their next event. These are potential clients, but they're not the ones you need the most! Charge these clients a smaller markup, but don't start out doing a bunch of free work, or you'll have more free work than you can handle.

Here are some key ways to find *paying* clients.

- **Set up a website.** If you don't have design skills yourself, use a template site like Weebly or Squarespace. List prices for your basic printing items (brochures, postcards, etc.) on the site, or even set up an online store.
- **List your business on Google Maps.** Why wouldn't you want to be on the most-searched search engine in the world? If you're working from home, you can hide your street address, but you'll still show up in local searches for print brokers or printing companies.
- **Let potential customers know you're there.** I once landed a small auto dealership as a client by sending them a simple letter

printed on an inkjet printer, offering 1000 business cards for $30. I think I mailed a total of 10-20 letters the same day, so for less than $10 in postage, I netted a client that has ordered many thousands of business cards as well as other materials for their dealership. In addition, the owner recommended me to a relative, who gave me the job of redoing all of the stationery for an accountant who was moving.

- **Go after low-hanging fruit.** There are a lot of customers "serious" print brokers don't go after. Authors, churches, and many small businesses end up spending huge amounts for printing at office supply stores because nobody asks for their business. Just show up at a writer's conference or a church event with a business card, and watch the business come your way!
- **Sell online.** Of course, sell from your website, but don't forget Ebay! With wholesale rates, you can still make money selling custom printed materials on the world's largest auction site. Just make your "Buy It Now" prices cover your cost, the Ebay fees, and shipping!
- **Use social media.** LinkedIn, Twitter, and Facebook are key to interacting with potential customers and selling "face to face." By posting interesting content and responding quickly to potential clients, you can score customers.

6

Finding Your Own Vendors

Remember — you are selling your knowledge and resources. You are the man or woman who knows where to get the printing done. But if you search online for "print shops," you'll find a million of them! How do you know where to go to find reputable, competitive printers for the products you sell?

After you have been in the business for awhile, you will begin to find your own resources. But for print brokers just starting out, I recommend that you look for a printer that is

- **Trade Only / Wholesale:** Several printers will have *wholesale* in their name or website. But you want to look for companies that sell to "trade only" — to those who are in the printing business. These printers charge a lower price to brokers than the general public can get.
- **High Quality Printing:** Your reputation is on the line, because most of your customers won't see the printing company on their invoice. They'll see your name. You want a company that will print quality work for your customers.
- **Affordable Pricing:** Pricing can vary substantially in the printing business. There's often a reason — certain locations for print shops have tax or labor advantages that allow companies located there to offer a lower price. Don't always pursue the lowest price — that's a recipe for terrible printing. But consider price; otherwise, you'll

make less profit or your customers will have to pay more.
- **Affordable and Fast Shipping:** Typically, shipping printed products via FedEx is more expensive than UPS, so I avoid using printers that use only FedEx. One of my local printers delivers for free, so for local jobs I often use them. Other than that, I try to use printers that are within one day ground shipping for the destination. Both Printograph and 4over (in the bonus section) have multiple locations across the United States and Canada, so they are easy choices. Sinalite is based in Canada, but can ship within 2-3 days to most US locations.

Where do you find these printers? You can find them online, in trade magazines, and at trade shows — or you can go to the **bonus section** in this book and find my personal recommendations based on thirteen years of experience in this industry.

7

Getting Paid

Many print shops will charge you up front for their products. And it makes sense for you to charge up front, too. Here's why:

Most of the people you work with *will pay you* — someday. Until then, you're left holding the bag. A credit card will give you up to thirty days before they start charging interest - but then the rate goes up. If you want to become a loan shark, go ahead. But if you want to be a print broker, charge up front.

You can make this easy by accepting credit cards through Square or Paypal, both easy services for entry level entrepreneurs to use.

> **STOP!** *Once your website is up and running, you will get requests and possibly orders for a huge number of banners or signs. The request will probably be made in broken English, and the products are usually requested to be shipped to a distant country, using a particular courier service. It's probably a scam. Once you process their payment and pay the "shipping company" (which is bogus) for the shipping, they won't pick up the order and you'll find out that the credit card you processed is stolen. You're going to have to eat the cost! So if an order appears suspicious or abnormal, don't accept it. Call the billing phone number and ask if it's a legitimate order.*

You can invoice through both Square and Paypal as well.

8

More than Just a Print Broker

Print brokers sell solutions, and those solutions are *more* than just printing. You can make more money by adding other services to your repertoire.

Direct Mail

As I write this, we are getting several mailings per day from political candidates. In fact, we have probably received ten pieces of mail each from two candidates in a hotly contested state house seat! Why? They think direct mail works.

After years of decline because of email, direct mail and direct mail response rates are increasing. This is good news for print brokers because *every single direct mail piece has to be printed!*

The United States Postal Service's "Every Door Direct Mail" program makes direct mail easy, affordable, and effective. You can blanket a community with mailers for less than 18 cents apiece (as of August 4, 2018).

Graphic Design

Printed materials have to be designed, and you can offer design services along with the printed products you offer.

If you have an eye and the skill for it, do it yourself! In the resource section in the back, I list helpful programs, some for free, that you can use.

If you can't do design yourself, find some graphic designers to do design jobs for you. Use freelance job boards, Craigslist, and Fiverr.com to find designers for simple jobs.

Web Design

Web design is a specialized field requiring skills that can be self-taught or learned in a community college. If you offer web design, I recommend that you require customers to host their own sites and make sure you use a platform like Wordpress that allows customers (or you, for a fee) to update their own sites.

Sign and Wrap Installation

Sign installation may require licensing and knowledge of local permits. Check with local authorities to make sure. You may want to find a local sign installer and ask (even pay!) to tag along on a few jobs to get the hang of things.

Installing vehicle wraps is a specialized skill that can be lucrative, if it's done right. I recommend getting training through Avery or 3m, two of the market leaders in the field.

9

Quick Start: 10 Steps to Starting Your Print Broker Business

I cannot offer legal or accounting advice. The steps below are steps that I took to become a business, but they may differ from locality to locality, and I recommend that you check your local requirements first.

1. Register your business name with your state. This is usually done at the county level. Check with the Small Business Administration to find out the rules for your state. (I registered as a sole proprietor, easier for tax and record-keeping purposes for me.)
2. Register with the IRS to receive your Federal Employer Identification Number. This will be your sales tax identification number in many states.
3. File for a state sales tax permit. The TaxJar blog has a helpful guide to where to file for each state.
4. Register your domain name. I use **NameSilo** because they have the lowest domain renewal prices I've found.
5. Set up an official email address, like "Joe@JoesPrinting.com. You can do this through NameSilo and forward it to your current address.
6. Open financial accounts. You'll probably need a bank account, as well as online payment accounts like Paypal or Square.
7. Begin applying for trade pricing to the printers in the "Resources"

section of this book.
8. Set up your website. If website design isn't your thing, use a designer like Weebly or SquareSpace to get a beautiful website up in minutes.
9. Get some customers!
10. Make money!

10

Preparing Files for Printing

I leave you with one last and important word about preparing files for printing. Always, always follow the guidelines from the printer for final preparation of files. Each printer will have different specifications. Here are some things to watch for:
1. Format: Most printers are happy with a PDF (portable document file). This is the easiest file to use across all platforms. But make sure the PDF is flattened and outlined, first!
2. Color Space: You usually have the option in creating a file to do it in CMYK or RGB. Most printing companies will want it in CMYK, since that is the traditional ink colors. The exception: some large-format printers will request RGB files, since large format printers have a wider color gamut. Check with the printer first!
3. Bleed: When in doubt, leave at least .125" bleed around the file. Most printers prefer bleed. Some large format printers request files without it.
4. Resolution: For small format printing (postcards, books), 300 dpi is acceptable for photos. For large format printing (banners, signs), 150 dpi is usually acceptable. View PDF files at 100% size to ensure correct resolution.

After thirteen years in this business, including five at a large format printer, improperly prepared files are the bane of a printer's existence. Make sure your files are prepared correctly!

II

Bonus Section: Resources for Print Brokers

A guide to print shops, software, and other resources for beginning print brokers

11

Offset Printing

The print shops below mostly use "gang run" printing. That means they "gang up" multiple print jobs and print them together for efficiency, allowing them to do smaller jobs at a competitive price. For all except the most extreme color-critical jobs, the shops below do excellent work.

The sites below will all require proof that you are truly a print broker. Before you apply for print broker pricing, you will need your business license (usually obtained from the county) and your state sales tax license.

Printograph.com

This is the trade-only branch of GotPrint.com, a major retail printing site. Printograph offers very low trade-only pricing and shipping from several locations in the United States and Canada. They offer offset printing as well as large format printing.

4over.com

One of the major players in trade-only printing, 4over offers almost every imaginable printed product as well as a robust rewards program. 4over also has multiple North American locations.

Sinalite.com

This is a recent addition to my printing portfolio that has provided me with excellent customer service, low prices, and fast shipping. Their selection rivals Printograph and 4over, and their fast and low-priced shipping is a huge advantage. They are based in Canada.

ColorPointPrint.com

For basic printed materials, ColorPointPrint offers quality work and fast turnaround. An added bonus for me is that they offer delivery in the Metro Detroit area. They also offer screenprinted envelopes.

AllProColor.com

AllProColor is also based in the Metro Detroit area, but ships all over North America. They offer union-label printing as well as some same day printing options. They have been very helpful, especially on date-sensitive materials.

DFSFullColor.com

DFS is a full-service printer that offers a great selection of quality products and an excellent guarantee.

12

Large Format Print Vendors

Large format printers print banners, yard signs, vehicle magnets, and more. Here are some of my favorites:

Signs2Trade
Based in Brighton, Michigan, Signs2Trade offers incredible trade pricing as well as 24-hour turnaround on most products!

Signs365
Also in Michigan, Signs365 brags that they are "only trade only." They offer a wide variety of large format products, and offer free "overnight shipping" on most products for $10!

Digital Print Solutions
This Minnesota company caters to resellers only and offers vehicle graphics as well as banners, yard signs, and magnets.

B2Sign
Based in California, B2Sign has a wide large format selection, and especially good pricing on display products like banner stands, table throws, and backdrops.

Sign4Trade

Also based in California, Sign4Trade offers great deals, especially on large banners.

13

Specialty Printing

Books

Print-on-demand publishing makes it possible for self-published authors to print, literally, one book at a time! Check out CreateSpace (from Amazon), Lulu, and Diggypod.

Carbonless Forms

I recommend CarbonlessonDemand or NCRForms.com.

CDs and Digital Media

Trepstar.com provides custom printed CDs and packaging.

Promotional Products

For custom promotional products, check out DistributorCentral or QualityLogoProducts.

14

Software Suggestions

Design Software

The Adobe Creative Suite is the most commonly used design software, but it is very expensive. If you're starting out, you may wish to start out with something less expensive up front. For years, I have used Art Explosion Publisher Pro. The name sounds cheesy, but it is truly one of the most fully featured software packages I have used.

I haven't used Affinity yet, but it is much cheaper than Adobe with similar functionality.

Billing Software

I use Express Invoice, which is free for small companies. It provides easy record-keeping and reporting features.

15

Design Resources

Being a print broker will necessarily involve some basic design and layout resources. Here are some I have found helpful:

Envato Market
From stock graphics to brochure templates, Envato Market has a huge library of themes and templates to purchase.

Adobe Stock
For about $30/month, you can get 10 professional images, and even basic logo templates.

MakerBook
This is probably the only free resource I need to give you. MakerBook has a directory of free design resources including stock photography, vector images, product display graphics, and more!

About the Author

Tim Miller is the founder and owner of Miller Design Studio, a small graphic design business based in Detroit, Michigan. He has worked for over 13 years in the printing industry, including five years as a digital printer in Canton, Michigan. He lives with his wife Heather in the Brightmoor neighborhood of Detroit, Michigan. He welcomes your comments and questions at printbroker@millerdesignstudio.net.